MCLAREN • ASTON MARTIN • JAGUAR

Paul Mason

W
FRANKLIN WATTS
LONDON • SYDNEY

Franklin Watts
First published in Great Britain in 2017 by
The Watts Publishing Group

Executive editor: Adrian Cole
Series designer: Mayer Media
Design manager: Peter Scoulding
Picture researcher: Diana Morris

Photo acknowledgements:
Alizada Studios/Shutterstock: 4-5c, 31b. Ascari:
7c, 7t. Aston Martin: back cover, 1b, 3c, 12-
13c, 13t, 8t, 10-11, 13t, 28t. BAC: 28c. Pieter
Beens/Shutterstock. 27t. Columbia/EON/Da/
REX/Shutterstock: 17t. Mike Dodd/McLaren
Automotive: 24-25c. Jaguar: front cover t, 28b,
29t. Sergey Kohl/Shutterstock: 5t. Radoslaw
Lecyk/Shutterstock: 30cr. Lotus Cars: 3t, 3b,
18-19t, 19b, 20-21c, 21t. Magic Car Pics/REX/
Shutterstock: 5b. McLaren Automotive: front
cover b, 22-23b, 25b, 29cr, 29cl, 32. Noble Cars:
26-27c. Rachel Palmer/Aston Martin: 8-9b.
Sotheby's: 30cl. Maskim Toome/Shutterstock:
15t. TVR: 29b. Miro Vrlik Photography/
Shutterstock: 14-15c. CC Wikimedia: 30t,
30bl,30br. Vande Wolf Images/Dreamstime: 1t,
16-17. Aleksandr Zavatskiy/Dreamstime: 23c.

Kevlar® is a registered trademark of
E. I. du Pont de Nemours and Company

ISBN 978 1 4451 5141 0

Printed in China

Franklin Watts
An imprint of
Hachette Children's Group
Part of The Watts Publishing Group
Carmelite House
50 Victoria Embankment
London EC4Y 0DZ

An Hachette UK Company
www.hachette.co.uk

www.franklinwatts.co.uk

FSC
www.fsc.org

MIX
Paper from
responsible sources
FSC® C104740

Contents

Words highlighted in **bold** can be found in the glossary

Ever since cars were invented in the late 1800s, British companies have been building high-performance, expensive, sometimes impractical cars. But in 1961, Jaguar released a car that became probably the world's most famous fast car: the Jaguar E-Type.

THE BIG THREE

Jaguar still makes supercars. So do two other big British companies: Aston Martin and McLaren. McLaren is famous for producing cars that use Formula 1 technology on the road. Aston Martin and Jaguar are famous for GT, or 'Grand Tourer', models. These are designed to cover long distances in comfort — but very, very quickly.

Several other British companies make high-performance cars. Some, like Ascari, make true supercars, while companies such as Lotus make cars that can be adapted for racing. Others, like TVR, have struggled to stay in business.

What's it like to ~~drive?~~ look at?

The most beautiful car in the world.

— Enzo Ferrari (yes, THAT Enzo, the one who founded Ferrari) speaking about the Jaguar E-Type

Leather race-car-style **bucket seats** in early E-Types were later replaced by more comfortable seats

Each wheel has its own independent suspension system

The Jaguar E-Type was the first British supercar. It was based on the D-Type racing car, which won the Le Mans 24-hour endurance race in 1955, 1956 and 1957.

Disc brakes on all four wheels were race-car technology in 1961

Price Tag...

E-TYPE TIMELINE

1961
Jaguar E-Type appears at the Geneva Motor Show. Demand for test drives is so high that a second car is driven from the Jaguar factory in Coventry to Geneva in one night.

1964
Engine size is increased to 4200 cc

1968
Series 2 E-Type is released, with many changes to fit in with US safety regulations

1971
Series 3 E-Type, with a 5300 cc V12 engine; production stops in 1975

Start saving! The most expensive E-Types are the Series 1 Lightweights. Only 12 were ever made, and in 2015 one of them was sold for almost £6 million. Even an 'ordinary' Series 1 costs more than most houses.

The Aston Martin DB4, launched in 1958, was the quickest production car of its time.

JUST WHAT *IS* A SUPERCAR?

There is no exact definition of what makes a supercar. But most supercars share some of these features:

- Expensive
- Made in small numbers
- High-performance in every area of their design
- Very fast, and probably very light
- Tricky to drive
- Useless for bringing home a week's shopping, going on a camping trip, taking kids to school, etc.

Four-speed manual gearbox has no **synchromesh** on first gear – which makes using first and second gear a real challenge

Glass-covered headlights featured on early E-Types

The 1958 TVR Grantura had a fibreglass body, and helped to launch the TVR company.

TOP SPEED

240 kph
(150 mph)

0–100 KPH

7 seconds

MAX POWER

198 kW
266 **bhp** @ 5,500 rpm

MAX TORQUE

325 Nm
240 ft/lb @ 4,000 rpm

	Max RPM: **not known**
	Engine: **3800 cc inline 6**
	Weight: **1,315 kg**
	Fuel use per 100 km (estimated): **13.3 litres**
	CO$_2$: **not known**
	Gearbox: **4-speed manual**
	Drive: **rear wheels**
	Main body: **steel**
	Frame: **steel**
	Braking: **steel**

ASCARI
KZ1

Ascari is named after Alberto Ascari, an Italian racing driver. He was the first person ever to win the Formula 1 World Championship more than once. You would expect a car from a company like that to be fast – and the KZ1 is definitely fast.

The owner of Ascari is a rich Dutch businessman called Klaas Zwart. He was once described as, "the biggest **petrolhead** in the world." Zwart designed the KZ1 to be as simple and lightweight as possible, without the electronic driver aids used in many supercars. If you start to skid in a KZ1, the car's computer will not help you!

THE KZ1-R
Ascari also produces a racing version of the KZ1, the KZ1-R. The inside is almost completely stripped out. There are no electric windows, no comfortable seats (just lightweight carbon fibre ones), no leather trim and no carpets. But, the KZ1-R is so lightweight that it speeds off as quickly as a Lamborghini Murcielago LP640.

THE ASCARI RACE RESORT
In 2002, Ascari opened its own racetrack in southern Spain. Buying a KZ1 gives you the right to use the 5.5 km circuit, and drivers can also try the Ascari LMP900 racing car.

Rear **spoiler** automatically comes up at 80 kph, giving the back tyres extra grip

Side vents channel air to the engine, cooling it and providing oxygen. The oxygen is needed so the engine can burn vast amounts of fuel

Engine is based on a BMW M5's, but with most parts changed or adapted. The KZ1 has almost 30 per cent more power

What's it like to drive?
One of the finest-handling supercars of this or any generation. No Ferrari made today steers as well as this, no Porsche can match its blend of ride and refinement.

– review on autocar.co.uk

KZ1 TIMELINE

2000
Ascari starts taking orders for the KZ1

Ascari first reveals the KZ1 concept car

2004 2005
The first KZ1s are delivered; the KZ1-R is announced

Price Tag...
When it was launched in 2005, the KZ1 cost a minimum of £235,000, more if you added extras. Only a few have ever been made, and used cars very rarely come up for sale.

The KZ1-R* is the race car version of the design. It is lighter and more powerful than the normal car — but not as comfortable.

Entire body apart from doors and bumpers is made of lightweight carbon fibre

OU04 VOG

TOP SPEED
322 kph
(200 mph)

0–100 KPH
3.9 seconds

MAX POWER
373 kW
500 bhp @ 7,000 rpm

MAX TORQUE
499 Nm
368 ft/lb @ 4,500 rpm

Max RPM:
7,250

Engine:
4941 cc V8

Weight:
1,275 kg

Fuel use per 100 km:
not known

CO_2:
not known

Gearbox:
6-speed manual

Drive:
rear wheels

Main body:
carbon fibre

Frame:
carbon fibre

Braking:
steel

NAME: Alberto Ascari
LIVED: 1918–55
FAMOUS AS: Racing driver

Ascari started as a motorbike racer before switching to cars. In 1952 he won the Formula 1 World Championship driving a Ferrari. He won a second championship, again in a Ferrari, in 1953. As an Italian driving an Italian car, Ascari became a national hero.

* The 'R' is for Rebel.

ASTON MARTIN
VANTAGE GT12

The GT12 is what you get when you take "the most ferocious Aston Martin ever produced", and make it MORE ferocious!

The GT12 is based on a V12 Vantage S. The Vantage S comes with a monstrous V12 engine, but is also Aston Martin's lightest car. But Aston decided it was not light enough. They shaved 100 kg off the weight – which is the same as telling a heavy passenger to get out and walk. They made it lower and wider than any other Vantage. And they gave it different **aerodynamics**, with a bigger front **splitter** and a special rear **wing**.

The GT12 is very different from many supercars. In a Gumpert Apollo Enraged, for example, the noise of the engine is practically deafening – some drivers wear earplugs while driving one! The Vantage S is amazingly quiet by comparison. Almost no road noise reaches the driver – just the noise of the engine and exhaust roaring and crackling.

Factory: Gaydon, Warwickshire

The GT12 features an upgraded Vantage engine, with lightweight magnesium parts.

Price Tag...

Only 100 GT12s were ever made, and they were all sold long ago. Buying one would have cost you £250,000 – which is £120,000 more than a 'standard' V12 Vantage S. (Put another way, that's an extra £1,200 for each kg of weight lost.)

Much of the GT12's frame and **bodywork** is stuck together using glue

Carbon-fibre front splitter and rear wing improve aerodynamics

VANTAGE GT12 TIMELINE

2005 — The first Vantage is released

2013 — V12 Vantage S, lighter and more powerful than any previous Vantage

2015 — Aston Martin announce they will make 100 Vantage GT12s, a track-influenced version of the V12 Vantage S

What's it like to drive?

*A wonderful, characterful machine… That monstrous engine (and its soundtrack) dominates proceedings but dig deeper and you'll find brakes and **chassis** to match.*

– review on carmagazine.co.uk

Engine is front-mid mounted: in front of the driver, but behind the front wheels

Separate suspension system for each wheel

TOP SPEED
330 kph
(205 mph)

0–100 KPH
3.5 seconds

MAX POWER
441 kW
(592 bhp) @ 7,000 rpm

MAX TORQUE
625 Nm
(461 lb/ft) @ 5,500 rpm

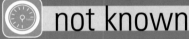

Max RPM:
not known

Engine:
5935 cc V12

Weight:
1,565 kg

Fuel use per 100 km:
14.3 litres

CO2:
323 g/km

Gearbox:
7-speed automatic

Drive:
rear wheels

Main body:
carbon fibre

Frame:
aluminium

Braking:
carbon-ceramic

ASTON MARTIN
V12 ZAGATO

'Zagato' is a name Aston Martin gives cars it makes with the help of the Zagato factory in Italy. And Italy, as every car fan knows, is where supercars originally came from.*

Factory: Gaydon, Warwickshire

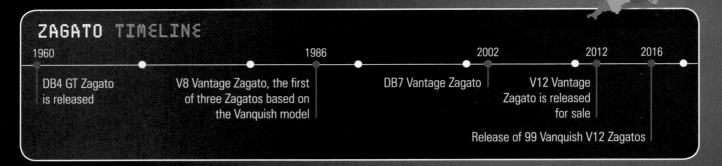

ZAGATO TIMELINE

1960	1986	2002	2012	2016

DB4 GT Zagato is released

V8 Vantage Zagato, the first of three Zagatos based on the Vanquish model

DB7 Vantage Zagato

V12 Vantage Zagato is released for sale

Release of 99 Vanquish V12 Zagatos

THE FIRST ZAGATO

The first Zagato was the DB4 GT Zagato – one of the rarest cars Aston Martin ever built: only 19 were made. When it was released in 1960 it cost £5,470. This was a lot of money, but today you could sell one for several million pounds!

THE V12 ZAGATO

The V12 Zagato was built to celebrate 50 years of the two companies working together. It is a more powerful, lighter version of an Aston Martin Vantage. The outside panels are all hand-made using a combination of aluminium and carbon fibre for lightness. Its 5935 cc V12 engine spits the Vantage Zagato to 100 kph in about 4 seconds. This is an amazing speed for a luxury car that can be driven hundreds of kilometres in complete comfort.

Front splitter channels air to improve the Zagato's aerodynamics

'Sport' button on dashboard makes the engine respond more quickly and the exhaust more noisy

Huge front grille allows cooling air to flow into the engine space

*Most people think the Lamborghini Miura, which appeared in 1966, was the first supercar.

TOP SPEED
305 kph
(190 mph)

0–100 KPH
4.2 seconds

MAX POWER
380 kW
(510 bhp) @ 6,500 rpm

MAX TORQUE
570 Nm
(420lb/ft) @ 5,750 rpm

Price Tag...

Forget it, if you want a new one: only 150 were made and they were quickly sold. The basic car cost £330,000 plus tax – which in the UK meant it cost £396,000.

What's it like to drive?

Putting such a big engine in such a small car makes it an absolute hooligan to drive ... whether you're gazing at it on your driveway or pelting across the countryside, you'll be grinning away madly as it gets your adrenaline pumping.

– review on *autoexpress.com*

NAME: Ugo Zagato
LIVED: 1890–1968
FAMOUS AS: Founder of Zagato **coachworks**

As a teenager, Zagato moved from Italy to Germany to work in a coachworks. He later returned to Italy, and during World War I worked building lightweight aircraft. When the war ended, Zagato began building lightweight racing-car bodies for the Alfa Romeo racing team. Over the years since, Zagato's company has built special cars for Alfa Romeo, Jaguar, Spyker, Lamborghini, Ferrari and Aston Martin.

Fixed rear wing adds **downforce**, giving the rear wheels better grip

Max RPM:
not known

Engine:
5935 cc V12 non-turbo

Weight:
1,680 kg

Fuel use per 100 km:
14.3 litres

CO2:
388 g/km

Gearbox:
6-speed manual

Drive:
rear wheels

Main body:
carbon fibre and aluminium

Frame:
alloy

Braking:
carbon-ceramic

ASTON MARTIN
DB11

Any car that comes fitted with 'launch control' HAS to be good! That's what Formula 1 cars have – space rockets, too. And so does the Aston Martin DB11.

BETTER THAN 007

This is the car that James Bond drove in *Spectre* – but better! Bond's car was a DB10, which Aston Martin built specially for the film. The DB10 was actually a **tricked-out** version of the DB9. Only two show-car DB10s were built. In 2016 one of them was sold at an auction for £2.4 million.

The DB11 is the replacement for the DB9. It is one of the first modern Aston Martins to use turbo chargers. These whoosh extra air into the engine, feeding it more oxygen. The extra oxygen is used to burn more fuel, creating more power.

Factory: Gaydon, Warwickshire

What's it like to drive?

The V12 howls that pure, complex tone and throttle response is excellent … it massively out punches the [DB9's] engine on corner exits and gives the rear tyres a really hard time.

– review of a prototype DB11 on *evo.co.uk*

DB11 TIMELINE

1963	1994	2004	2016
The DB5 is released. A year later a gadget-filled version (with an ejector passenger seat, machine guns in the front bumpers and a bullet-proof rear panel!) appears in the James Bond film *Goldfinger*. The DB5 soon becomes every schoolchild's dream car.	DB7, the first modern DB-model car. Two racing versions are built; despite being stripped down racing cars, they have leather interiors because Aston Martin wants them to be 'gentleman racers'.	The first DB9s are released for sale. The DB9 is the last DB with a non-turbo engine.	The DB11 goes on sale at the end of the year

'Gills' on the side release air from the wheel arch, improving front-wheel grip and keeping the brakes cool.

The DB11 is a 2+2, which means there is just enough room for two small (or very scrunched-up) passengers in the back

Above 155 kph, a rear spoiler is automatically activated

Air is channelled through DB11's body. It is released from slots in the boot lid, improving aerodynamics

Suspension can be set to GT, Sport and Sport+ modes. These are for rough roads; smooth, fast roads; or racetracks

Price Tag...

Prices start at £154,900 for the cheapest DB11, but adding extras means most cars will actually cost more.

FROM V12 TO INLINE 6

When the engine's whole power is not needed, one side of the V12 engine shuts down completely. The engine becomes an inline 6, which reduces the amount of fuel the car uses and the amount of pollution it creates.

TOP SPEED

322 kph

(200 mph)

0–100 KPH

3.9 seconds

MAX POWER

447 kW

600 bhp @ 6,500 rpm

MAX TORQUE

700 Nm

516 ft/lb @ 1,500 rpm

 Max RPM:
7,000

 Engine:
5200 cc twin-turbo V12

 Weight:
1,770 kg

 Fuel use per 100 km:
11.8 litres (est.)

 CO2:
270 g/km (est.)

 Gearbox:
8-speed automatic

 Drive:
rear wheels

 Main body:
aluminium

 Frame:
carbon fibre

Braking:
carbon-ceramic

JAGUAR
F-TYPE SVR

Factory: Birmingham, West Midlands

When it went on sale in 2016, the F-Type SVR became the fastest production car Jaguar had ever made. This 320 kph rocket ship is part of a long line of fast Jaguars that goes back to the E-Type (see pages 4–5).

Jaguar's F-Type appeared in 2013. It was the company's first 2-seater sports car since the E-Type. The SVR version of the F-Type turns the dial up to 'supercar'. It is lighter, more powerful and faster than any other road-going Jaguar.

SPECIAL VEHICLE OPERATIONS

The F-Type SVR was designed by Jaguar's brilliantly named 'Special Vehicle Operations' team. This unit makes the most extreme Jaguars possible. The F-Type SVR (which is short for Special Vehicle Race), with its wider front end for enhanced aerodynamics and titanium exhaust, is the first Jaguar to be souped up by SVO.

Price Tag...

It will cost you anything from £110,000. Raid the extras list for things like carbon-ceramic brakes, black wheels and carbon-fibre extras, and the bill will be thousands more. Even the umbrella holder costs extra – and doesn't include an umbrella!

The carbon-fibre rear wing automatically lifts to improve grip at 112 kph (or when the driver puts the SVR into 'Dynamic' driving mode). It increases downforce by 15 per cent

Lightweight alloy wheels

Titanium exhaust is lighter and sounds different from the standard F-Type exhaust

Air flows through the engine bay, under the car's smooth floor and out through the rear splitter

F-TYPE SVR TIMELINE

1961	1975	2013	2016
Jaguar E-Type is released, and immediately becomes a sensation around the world	Jaguar stops production of the E-Type	F-Type is released for sale	SVR model takes the F-Type into supercar territory

As well as a coupe, the SVR comes in a slightly more expensive convertible version. The convertible is not quite as fast, but is probably better for turning up at parties, Oscars ceremonies, the MOBOs, etc.

322 kph	(200 mph)
0–100 KPH **3.7** seconds	
MAX POWER **423** kW	(567 bhp) @ 6,500 rpm
MAX TORQUE **700** Nm	(516 lb/ft) @ 3,500 rpm

What's it like to drive?

The F-Type's signature scream [sounds] like an angry King Kong thumping his chest at several thousand beats per minute. It's an appropriate soundtrack for Jaguar's fastest-ever production car.

– review on caranddriver.com

Vents in the front wings release air from the wheel arches, making the SVR more aerodynamic

Max RPM:
6,750

Engine:
5000 cc supercharged V8

Weight:
1,705 kg

Fuel use per 100 km:
11 litres

CO2:
269 g/km

Gearbox:
8-speed automatic

Drive:
all 4 wheels

Main body:
aluminium

Frame:
aluminium

Braking:
steel

NAME:	Norman Dewis
LIVED:	1920–present
FAMOUS AS:	Chief test driver for Jaguar, 1952–1985

Dewis is most famous for an overnight drive between Coventry and Geneva in 1961. The new E-Type was so popular at the Geneva Motor Show that a second car was needed the next day, so Dewis drove it from the Jaguar factory in Coventry to Geneva in 13 hours.

When the motor show *Top Gear* tried to do the same thing in an F-Type SVR in 2016, they could not manage it. Dewis had got there faster 55 years before!

C-X75

When you take the company that makes the F-Type SVR, and add it together with the Williams Formula 1 team, what do you get?

The Jaguar C-X75, that's what.

THE PHEV SUPERCAR

PHEV stands for Plug-in Hybrid Electric Vehicle. PHEV cars get some of their power from a petrol engine and some from an electric battery. They are not unusual: most big car companies make at least one. Not many can do over 350 kph, though!

As well as electric power, the C-X75 uses a little 1600 cc engine inspired by Formula 1 cars. (The Williams F1 team helped Jaguar develop the C-X75.) The engine is supercharged until it reaches 5,500 rpm, as supercharging works best at low rpm. Then it switches to being turbocharged, as this works better once the engine is working faster.

MOVIE-STAR CAR

The C-X75 is an A-list movie star car. It features in the Bond movie *Spectre*, racing through the streets of Rome alongside an Aston Martin DB10.

Battery pack behind the driver can be charged by being plugged in

Exhaust noise can be controlled by the driver, who can open or close flaps in the exhaust to change the noise

Grip is increased by the way air flows under the car and out the back. Gases flowing from the exhausts are also used to increase grip

What's it like to drive?

*The shriek of the **supercharger** builds and builds until … 5,500 rpm [when] it's only the turbo forcing air through the engine … then the deep snarl and growl of the exhausts really takes over and starts to deafen you.*

– review on *carmagazine.co.uk*

Price Tag…

It's not going to happen. In 2010 Jaguar originally built five C-X75s, none of which went on sale. A year later they said 250 would be built and sold — but then in 2012 announced that a shortage of likely buyers meant the C-X75 would not yet be released.

C-X75 TIMELINE

2010   2011   2012   2015

A specially built C-X75 races through the streets of Rome in the Bond movie *Spectre*

Jaguar decides not to offer the C-X75 for sale, but carries on working on the car

Jet power is dropped in favour of a small, Formula 1 type petrol engine

Jaguar shows off a jet-powered C-X75 at the Paris Motor Show

A C-X75 with headlights blazing as it chases an Aston Martin DB10 in the movie Spectre.

TOP SPEED

324 kph
(220 mph)

0–100 KPH

3.4 seconds

MAX POWER

634 kW
(850+ bhp) @ 9,700 rpm

MAX TORQUE

1000 Nm
(738 lb/ft) @ 3,000 rpm

Engine fitted with an ECO **stop-start system**

Max RPM:
10,200

Engine:
1600 cc
inline 4 turbo supercharged; 2 electric motors

Weight:
1,350 kg

Fuel use per 100 km:
9.6 litres

CO2:
not known*

Gearbox:
7-speed

Drive:
all 4 wheels

Main body:
cabon fibre

Frame:
cabon-fibre **monocoque**

Braking:
carbon-ceramic

When the brakes are used, the energy of the braking force is stored then used to power the electric motors (like a Formula 1 car's **KERS** system)

Gear shifts can be fully automatic, or controlled by the driver using steering-wheel paddles

Front grille and brake-cooling vents open only when needed. When they are closed, the C-X75 is more aerodynamic

*zero on electric power

EXIGE 360 CUP

Factory: Hethel, Norfolk

The Exige is a tiny, lightweight, supercharged bundle of fun. Compared to massive-engined supercars like the Lamborghini Aventador, the Exige is not very powerful. But the car has such a simple design, and weighs so little, that it is super-exciting to drive.

WEIGHT VS PERFORMANCE

All designers of fast cars have to make a decision: weight vs performance. For example, a small engine is lighter than a big one – but the big one is more powerful. A manual 6-speed gearbox is lighter than an 8-speed, twin-clutch automatic one – but the automatic will change gear more quickly. At Lotus, the weight of the car always comes first.

The 360 Cup is really a racing car that you can drive on the road. It is a more luxurious version of the race-track-only V6 Cup R. The designers did not have a massive challenge to make it more luxurious – the V6 does not even have a passenger seat. The 360 Cup also has air conditioning, and even carpets on (part of) the floor.

Rear spoiler automatically lifts when the car reaches 120 kph

Rear wing and splitter both increase downforce

Side vents channel air to the supercharged engine

The car's control system has four settings: Drive, Sport, Race and Off (which is only for really brave drivers)

NAME:	Colin Chapman
LIVED:	1928–82
FAMOUS AS:	Founder of Lotus

Chapman began the Lotus car company in 1952. He once said that, "Adding power makes you faster in a straight line. Subtracting weight makes you faster everywhere." Ever since, Lotus designers have preferred light weight to high power.

Chapman started a Formula 1 team in 1958. His lightweight, mid-engined cars were less powerful than rivals Ferrari and Maserati, but handled much better and used new technology. In the 1960s and 1970s, Lotus won seven Constructors' Championships and six Drivers' Championships.

Price Tag...

For a supercar, this is cheap! Prices start at £63,000 – you could buy six of these instead of a V12 Vantage Zagato, and still have enough money left for a trip to the cinema! Unfortunately, though, Lotus only made 50.

What's it like to drive?

Is it quick? Oh Lordy yes … you're fired up the road in double-quick time… It's brilliant.

– review on *carmagazine.co.uk*

The driver can set the suspension to be softer, to absorb bumps, or harder for racetracks or smooth roads

Front splitter channels air under and through car for maximum downforce

WCM 886

GB

The car interior comes with GRP sports seats, with Lotus stitching, and four-point harnesses as an added extra (where allowed).

TOP SPEED
274 kph
(170 mph)

0–100 KPH
3.8 seconds

MAX POWER
257 kW
344 bhp @ 7,000 rpm

MAX TORQUE
400 Nm
295 ft/lb @ 4,500 rpm

Max RPM:
7,100

Engine:
3500 cc   supercharged V8

Weight:
1,125 kg

Fuel use per 100 km:
10.1 litres

CO2:
235 g/km

Gearbox:
6-speed manual

Drive:
rear wheels

Main body:
fibreglass

Frame:
aluminium

Braking:
steel

EXIGE 360 CUP TIMELINE

1996
Lotus releases the Elise, a mid-engined convertible sports car

2000
The Exige Series 3 is released, a more powerful car with different bodywork

2012
The first Exige, based on the Elise, appears

LOTUS
3-ELEVEN

OK, this Lotus is more of a track car than a supercar. But the Lotus 3-Eleven goes 0–100 kph in 2.9 seconds – which is supercar fast. It is supercar impractical, too – it doesn't even have a roof!

Factory: Hethel, Norfolk

WHO NEEDS A WINDSCREEN, ANYWAY?

Speed like the Lotus 3-Eleven's would be exciting in any car. In a car without a windscreen, the fun factor is even bigger (unless it starts raining). The driver and passenger wear **full-face helmets**. They are only a little more sheltered from the wind and weather than motorbike racers.

RACE AND ROAD

Lotus makes two versions of the 3-Eleven, the Race and the Road. The Race is more powerful and a bit lighter, but is not really designed for driving on the road. On a racetrack, though, it goes like a bomb. Around the famous **Nürburgring** track, the 3-Eleven is almost as fast as a Porsche 918 Spyder. And in 2016, it actually did a lap of the Hockenheim Grand Prix track FASTER than the 918.

Carbon-fibre rear wing is adjustable on the Race version of the 3-Eleven; fixed in position on the Road version

Roll cage protects driver and passenger if the car turns over in an accident

Large rear wing, plus front and rear splitters, channel air flow to increase performance

LOTUS 3-ELEVEN TIMELINE

1956
Lotus Eleven, weighing just 400 kg, is launched; it wins at Le Mans and Sebring

2007
The 2-Eleven, a doorless open car based on the Lotus Elise, is released

2016
3-Eleven available for sale; Lotus plans to make just 311 cars

TOP SPEED
290* kph
(180 mph)

0–100 KPH
3.0* seconds

MAX POWER
343* kW
(460 bhp) @ 7,000 rpm

MAX TORQUE
525* Nm
387 ft/lb @ 3,500 rpm

Price Tag...

It will cost you £116,500 for the Race (and £82,500 for the Road). For a car that did a lap of the Nürburgring in 7:06, this is cheap! The fastest car around the course, the Porsche 918 Spyder, is 9 seconds faster – but it costs well over half a million pounds more.

At 240 kph the 3-Eleven Race's aerodynamics create 215 kg of downforce (the same as having a smallish bottlenose dolphin lying on the roof).

What's it like to drive?

[The speed is] so vicious and relentless. The initial kick forces the air from your lungs, which is instantly thrust back in [because] you're now doing 100 mph... I'm not sure I've felt acceleration quite like it in any other car I've driven.

– review on *topgear.com*

Splitter draws air in below nose of car

Per kilogram of weight, the 3-Eleven has almost the same amount of power as a Bugatti Veyron

---

Max RPM:
7,000+

Engine:
3500 cc supercharged V8

Weight:
890 kg

Fuel use per 100 km:
est. **10+ litres**

CO2:
est. **235 g/km**

Gearbox:
6-speed automatic

Drive:
rear wheels

Main body:
carbon

Frame:
aluminium

Braking:
steel

---

*for 3-Eleven Race (Road: 280 kph, 3.4 sec, 301 kW, 410 Nm)

P1

The F1 was McLaren's first ever supercar and the world's fastest production car. It won the Le Mans 24 Hour race (even though it hadn't been designed for racing) and was regularly voted the greatest car of all time.

So … McLaren had to do something REALLY special for their second supercar.

PARIS, 2012: THE P1 ON SHOW

In 2012, the McLaren stand at the Paris Motor Show was mobbed by car fans. At last, the company was showing the F1's replacement – the long-awaited P1 supercar.

The P1 features layer on layer of Formula 1 technology. Like the Jaguar C-X75, it is a PHEV, using a combination of petrol and electric power. The P1's hybrid-power motor is twice as powerful as an F1 car's KERS system. Its aerodynamics adapt to how and where the car is being driven, and it has computer-controlled suspension.

Price Tag...

Good luck – only 375 have been made. All of them were sold within months of the first orders being taken in 2013. (And that was even though prices started at £866,000.)

P1 V. LAFERRARI V. 918 SPYDER

The P1 only really has two rivals: the Ferrari LaFerrari and the Porsche 918 Spyder. In a test at Britain's Silverstone race circuit, the McLaren came out on top: 0.22 seconds ahead of the Porsche, and 0.34 seconds ahead of the Ferrari.

Roof snorkel sucks air into engine

Custom-made frame with built-in roll cage and door bars for protection

In Race mode, the P1 changes height. It drops 50 mm closer to the ground, and its suspension becomes 300 per cent stiffer

Rear wing has a **DRS** feature, which can be opened and closed using a button on the steering wheel

P1 TIMELINE

1992

McLaren F1 is released; 106 cars were made before production finished in 1998

2012

McLaren P1 is released

NAME: Gordon Murray
LIVED: 1946–present
FAMOUS AS: F1 and McLaren road car designer

Murray worked as a Formula 1 car designer and technical director between 1969 and 2006. He worked at McLaren's Formula 1 team between 1987 and 2006.

When the McLaren boss, Ron Dennis, decided the company should make a fast road car, Murray was put in charge of McLaren Cars. There he helped produce the F1 and the Mercedes Benz SLR McLaren supercars. He's now helping to develop a new car for TVR.

TOP SPEED
350 kph (electronically limited)
(226 mph)

0–100 KPH
2.8 seconds

MAX POWER
675 kW
905 bhp @ 7,500 rpm

MAX TORQUE
980 Nm
723 lb/ft @ 7,500 rpm

What's it like to drive?

Rest assured, thrill-seeking billionaires … you'd have to have lived a life in either Top Fuel dragsters or carrier-based fighter planes to grow [used to] this level of acceleration. It's never terrifying but always scary enough to remind you what an amazing car it is.

– review on *caranddriver.com*

The electric motor's power can be called on by pushing a button on the steering wheel

*The P1 GTR is a full-on race car version of the P1. It is more powerful and lighter. If you buy one of these, McLaren offers you driver training in a Formula 1 **simulator**!*

 Max RPM:
not known

 Engine:
3799 cc twin-turbo V8 electric motor

 Weight:
1,500 kg

 Fuel use per 100 km:
8.3 litres

 CO2:
134 g/km

 Gearbox:
7-speed dual-clutch automatic

 Drive:
rear wheels

 Main body:
carbon fibre

 Frame:
carbon-fibre monocoque

 Braking:
carbon-ceramic

650S

Factory: Woking, Surrey

This is a supercar you could drive every day. Your mum or dad could use it to drop you at school, or for going to work. They could even head for the gym or the supermarket – the 650S has a big luggage compartment (well, big for a supercar).

So, you COULD go to the shops in it – but why would you? Just starting the engine makes your stomach churn with fear and excitement! The 650S weighs only a bit more than a Lotus Exige 360 Cup, but it has more power than a Porsche 911 GT3. It reaches 100 kph in 3.0 seconds. If you can find somewhere it's allowed, the 650S will reach a top speed of 333 kph.

CARBON MONOCOQUE

At the heart of the 650S is its carbon-fibre monocoque. The rest of the car is built around this structure, which surrounds the driver and passenger. Aluminium frames are attached to the front and rear. These are then used to attach the engine, suspension and bodywork. The monocoque can be made in just four hours. This is amazing, considering the monocoque for the McLaren F1 (see page 29) took about 4,000 hours to make.

Special doors, typical of McLaren, tilt upward at the rear to let the driver and passenger climb out

Huge side vents channel air into the engine area, keeping it as cool as possible

V8 engine and suspension can be set to Normal, Sport and Track modes

Magnesium wheels reduce weight by 15 kg

What's it like to drive?

Holy moly is this car fast. [It accelerates with] the wallop of Thor's hammer, right up to the [8,500] rpm redline... And if the engine is close on perfect then the ride and handling is more than a match.

– review on *telegraph.co.uk*

650S TIMELINE

2011
McLaren 12C, the first supercar completely designed and built by the company since the F1

2014
The 650S replaces the 12C; McLaren also release a convertible version called the 650S Spider

Price Tag...
You can buy one, but only if you have a lot of money. McLaren aims to make about 1,500 of the 650S a year, with the price starting at £195,000.

Aerodynamic, carbon-fibre **mirror stalks** reduce weight and **drag**

Carbon fibre monocoque weighs just 75 kg: less than an average man

650S

When braking hard from over 95 kph, the air brake at the rear lifts to help slow down the 650S, reducing its stopping distance by up to 20 m.

McLaren

N700 MCL

TOP SPEED
333 kph
(210 mph)

0–100 KPH
3.0 seconds

MAX POWER
478 kW
641 bhp @ 7,250 rpm

MAX TORQUE
678 Nm
500 ft/lb @ 6,000 rpm

Max RPM:
8,500

Engine:
3799 cc twin-turbo V8

Weight:
1,330 kg

Fuel use per 100 km:
11.7 litres

CO2:
275 g/km

Gearbox:
7-speed dual-clutch automatic

Drive:
rear wheels

Main body:
carbon fibre

Frame:
carbon fibre monocoque

Braking:
carbon-ceramic

NOBLE
M600

> Noble is a supercar company that does things differently. Other supercar makers keep adding electronic driver aids such as anti-lock brakes, active suspension and adaptive aerodynamics. Noble refuses to fit almost any of them.

SMALL WEIGHT, BIG POWER

What every M600 does have is light weight (less than a Renault Clio) and huge power (almost twice as much as a Porsche 718 Boxster). Steering an M600 around a racetrack at high speed is a task for skilled drivers only. In fact, this car is so fierce that Noble did have to fit one electronic aid, **traction control**. This can be turned off – but it's not recommended! To stop it happening accidentally, the button is covered with the same flip-up cover used in a Tornado fighter jet.

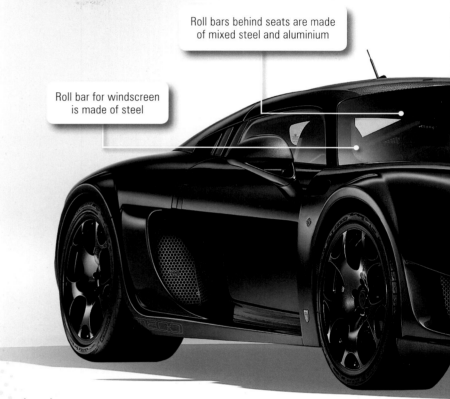

Roll bars behind seats are made of mixed steel and aluminium

Roll bar for windscreen is made of steel

What's it like to drive?

Raw, brain-mangling performance … not just in a straight line but also around corners, under brakes, during acceleration, everywhere and anywhere. What we are talking about is one of the fastest cars that has ever been built for use on the public road.

– review by *autocar.co.uk*

EVERY CAR A SPECIAL

Each M600 is a 'special'. Every one is hand built and adapted for the individual customer. Among the options is a 'Carbon Sport' body. All M600s have a carbon-fibre body, but the Carbon Sport is not painted. Instead, the carbon fibre is covered in clear, coloured lacquer. Noble claims to be the only supercar maker to offer this to its customers.

Price Tag...

When it was launched in 2009, prices started at £200,000. Many reviewers said they thought this was a bargain price for a car that went as fast as a McLaren F1. By 2016 prices had risen to £250,000 – still a bargain, just not quite such a big one!

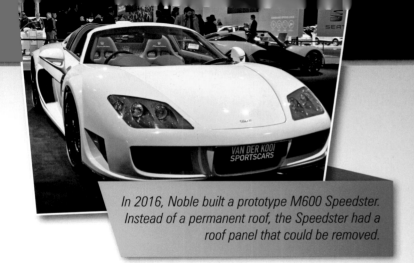

In 2016, Noble built a prototype M600 Speedster. Instead of a permanent roof, the Speedster had a roof panel that could be removed.

TOP SPEED
360 kph (est.)
(223 mph)

0–100 KPH
3.0 seconds

MAX POWER
492 kW
660 bhp @ 6,500 rpm

MAX TORQUE
819 Nm
604 ft/lb @ 3,800 rpm

Optional 'launch' control button: drivers push this when they want to do the fastest possible start

'Comfort' and 'sport' mode selector: sport is aimed at race tracks and smooth, fast roads

 Max RPM:
7,000

 Engine:
4439 cc V8 twin-turbo

 Weight:
1,198 kg

 Fuel use per 100 km:
11 litres (est.)

 CO2:
333 g/km

 Gearbox:
6-speed manual

 Drive:
rear wheels

 Main body:
carbon fibre

 Frame:
stainless steel

 Braking:
steel

M600 TIMELINE

2009 — The first M600s are released

2016 — Orders taken for the open-topped M600 Speedster

The supercars in this book are some of the newest, fastest and most exciting supercars made in Britain today. But lots of other fantastic British supercars have been manufactured. Here are a few of them:

MANUFACTURER: ASTON MARTIN
MODEL: ONE-77
YEAR: 2009

First glimpsed in 2008, shown at the Geneva Motor Show in 2009, the One-77 may be the greatest Aston Martin yet. Fitted with a 7300 cc V12 engine, it was voted the most beautiful supercar in several countries. Only 77 were ever made.

MANUFACTURER: BAC
MODEL: MONO
YEAR: 2012

One of the most extreme-looking road cars you will ever see; like a cross between a Formula 1 car and a fighter plane. So fast that, as one reviewer said: "The scenery disappears at a ridiculous rate when you put your foot down."

MANUFACTURER: JAGUAR
MODEL: XJR-15
YEAR: 1990

The world's first production car with a body and chassis made completely of carbon fibre. Only 53 were ever produced; the road version had indicators, bumpers and a slightly raised body so that it didn't get stuck on speed bumps.

MANUFACTURER: JAGUAR
MODEL: XJ-220
YEAR: 1992

For a brief moment in 1992, the XJ-220 was the coolest (and fastest) British supercar you could buy. Then the McLaren F1 was released, leaving the Jaguar looking a bit old-fashioned. Jaguar planned to make 1,500 but fewer than 300 were built, so the XJ-220 is a very rare car.

MANUFACTURER: MCLAREN
MODEL: F1
YEAR: 1992

Waiting for a plane after the 1988 Italian Grand Prix, four bigwigs from the McLaren Formula 1 team came up with a plan. They would build the best supercar the world had ever seen. It took four years, but when it was released the F1 became the fastest road car the world had ever seen. Only 106 were made.

MANUFACTURER: MCLAREN
MODEL: 12C
YEAR: 2011

The 12C was a long wait for McLaren fans. It was the first production car McLaren had designed and built since it stopped making the F1 in 1998. Fortunately, it was worth the wait. With a 3800 cc V8 engine and a body and frame made mostly of carbon fibre, the 12C can do almost 350 kph.

MANUFACTURER: TVR
MODEL: SAGARIS
YEAR: 2005

They wouldn't be allowed to make this car any more. TVR thought that safety features, such as **airbags,** made drivers too confident — so they didn't fit any. This is a car that has more power than most drivers can handle.

British car makers have always made small, fast 2-seater cars. These were usually called 'sporting' or 'sports cars'. The Jaguar E-Type on pages 4–5 is probably the most famous. Here are just a few of the other historical British supercars.

MANUFACTURER: MG
MODEL: T SERIES
YEAR: 1936

These little two-seat cars had a steel body built on a wooden frame (a technique also used by Morgan). In 1936 they cost £222 (about £4,000 in today's money). The MG-TC model became popular in the USA after the Second World War (1939–45). American soldiers liked the cars, which were not like anything you could buy in the USA.

MANUFACTURER: JAGUAR
MODEL: XK-120
YEAR: 1949

The '120' stood for 120 mph (193 kph), which was the speed the XK-120 could reach. That may not sound supercar fast today – but back in 1949, it made the Jag the fastest road car you could buy.

MANUFACTURER: AUSTIN HEALEY
MODEL: 3000
YEAR: 1959

The 3000 managed to squeeze 185 kph out of its 2912 cc inline-6 engine – and it was so low to the ground that it felt a lot faster. The car raced (and won) at circuits around the world. When the Mini Cooper S appeared in 1963, the 3000 became less popular as a racing car.

MANUFACTURER: LOTUS
MODEL: ELAN
YEAR: 1962

The Elan was a tiny little sports car with a steel frame and a fibreglass body. It was famous for its brilliant handling. When Gordon Murray finished the McLaren F1 design (see page 23), he apparently said he only had one disappointment. It was that the F1 didn't steer as well as a Lotus Elan.

MANUFACTURER: MORGAN
MODEL: PLUS 8
YEAR: 1968

Showing that some drivers like nothing more than some REALLY old-fashioned fun, the Plus 8 only stopped production in 2004. (One of Morgan's current designs, the 3-Wheeler, is descended from a car that was first made in 1911.)

UK

NATIONAL MOTOR MUSEUM

Beaulieu
Brockenhurst
Hampshire
SO42 7ZN

http://nationalmotormuseum.org.uk/
Supercars
and
www.beaulieu.co.uk
Not a specialist supercar museum, and focusing mainly on British cars, The National Motor Museum is still a great place for car fans to visit. Its website has details of special displays, which sometimes include supercars.

BRITISH MOTOR MUSEUM

Banbury Road
Gaydon
Warwickshire
CV35 0BJ

www.britishmotormuseum.co.uk
Like The National Motor Museum, many of the cars are British, but other countries' cars are also on display.

HAYNES MOTOR MUSEUM

Haynes International Motor Museum
Sparkford
Yeovil
Somerset
BA22 7LH

www.haynesmotormuseum.com
With one collection known as 'Supercar Century', this is a must-visit if you are nearby.

GOODWOOD FESTIVAL OF SPEED

Goodwood Estate
Chichester
West Sussex
PO18 0PX

www.goodwood.com
Held over one weekend each year in early summer, the Festival of Speed brings the latest, fastest, most super cars in the world together in one place. If you want to go, register for tickets early because this event always sells out.

JAGUAR VISITOR CENTRE, SOLIHULL

Jaguar Land Rover, Lode Lane, Solihull, West Midlands, B92 8NW

JAGUAR VISITOR CENTRE, CASTLE BROMWICH

Chester Road, Castle Vale, Birmingham, B35 7RA

www.jaguar.co.uk
Both centres offer factory tours where you can see Jaguars (and Land Rover/ Range Rovers) being built.

LOTUS FACTORY

Potash Lane
Hethel, Norwich
Norfolk
NR14 8EZ

www.lotuscars.com
The Lotus factory offers visitor tours that combine the story of the Lotus company (which started as one man working in a shed) with showing visitors how a modern Lotus is built.

aerodynamics how air flows around an object

airbag balloon that inflates when a car is in an accident, cushioning the driver or passengers

bodywork the outer shell of a vehicle

bhp short for brake horsepower, an alternative unit of power to kW

bucket seat seat with a rounded back that fits around your sides, holding you in place when going round a corner at high speed

chassis frame

coachworks maker of specialist car parts, particularly the outside panels

downforce downward pressure on the tyres, which makes them grip the road better

drag air resistance

DRS short for Drag Reduction System, which controls the angle of a car's rear wing to increase top speed

full-face helmet crash helmet that covers your whole head and face, right down to your chin

inline 6 engine with 6 cylinders in a row; Jaguar's inline 6 was in development since 1947

KERS short for Kinetic Energy Recovery System, a way of storing a car's braking force

manual gears a driver has to change for herself, using a gearstick

mirror stalk part that attaches a side-view mirror to a vehicle

monocoque object that gets its strength from its outer layer, instead of a supporting frame or skeleton

petrolhead fan of anything fast and petrol-powered, but especially cars

Nürburgring famous racetrack in Germany, made partly of normal roads, where many supercar makers go to test their cars

simulator machine that is designed to allow you to practise for a real-world dangerous situation in a safe way

splitter feature that controls air flow at the front or rear of a car, usually as a way of improving downforce

spoiler wing at the back of a car that presses downward as air flows over it, improving the tyres' grip

stop-start system computer-controlled system for stopping a car when it is not moving, then restarting it again when the driver wants to move off. Stop-start systems are a way of saving fuel and causing less pollution

supercharger device for feeding extra air into an engine, which increases its power. A supercharger has the same effect as a turbocharger, but is powered in a different way

synchromesh gearbox technology that helps the driver move forward smoothly after putting the car into a new gear

traction control system for stopping a car's tyres losing grip

tricked out fully accessorised, with lots of non-factory upgrades

wing also called a 'spoiler', a wing at the back of a car uses air flow to press the back of the car downward, improving the tyres' grip